Bonnie Shemie

Houses of snow, skin and bones

Tundra Books

Native dwellings: the Far North

Published in Canada by Tundra Books, Montreal, Quebec H3Z 2N2

Published in the United States by Tundra Books of Northern New York, Plattsburgh, N.Y. 12901

Distributed in the United Kingdom by Ragged Bears Ltd., Andover, Hampshire SP11 9HX

Library of Congress Catalog Number: 89-50778

Canadian Cataloging in Publication Data

Shemie, Bonnie, 1949-
    Houses of snow, skin and bones

ISBN 0-88776-240-9 hardcover 5 4 3
ISBN 0-88776-305-7 softcover 5 4 3 2

(Issued also in French under title: *Maisons de neige, de pierres et d'os*. ISBN 0-88776-295-6)

1. Inuit – Canada-Dwellings-Juvenile literature. 2. Igloos – Juvenile literature. House – Juvenile literature. I. Title.

E99.E7S533 1989   j392'.39'008997   C89-090215-1

Design by Rolf Harder & Associates, Montreal

Printed in Hong Kong by the South China Printing Co. (1988) Ltd.

Also by Bonnie Shemie:

Houses of bark: Native dwellings of the woodland Indians
Houses of hide and earth: Native dwellings of the Plains Indians
Houses of wood: Native dwellings of the Northwest Coast
Mounds of earth and shell: Native dwellings of the Southeast
Houses of adobe: Native dwellings of the Southwest

Acknowledgments:
The author/illustrator is particularly grateful to Fred Bruemmer, Arctic explorer, photographer and author of *Seasons of the Eskimo* for his generous advice, to Norbert Schoenauer, author of *6000 Years of Housing, the Pre-Urban House* and professor of architecture, McGill University, for his comments and suggestions on the text and for information in the study *Toward the Design of Shelter Forms in the North* by Arnold Koerte, University of Manitoba. She also wishes to acknowledge the assistance of Toby Morantz of the Department of Anthropology and George Wenzel of the Department of Geography, McGill University; the libraries of McGill University; the McCord Museum and the National Film Board of Canada, all of Montreal. Also Kitty Glover of the Canadian Museum of Civilization; the National Photo Archives and the National Library, all of Ottawa.

The severest climate on earth

Winter in the Far North means months of darkness over deserts of ice in the coldest and driest weather known. Yet for thousands of years families have managed to live here, a miracle of survival. It would have been impossible if they had not been able to build shelters with whatever was to hand: snow, earth, stones, animal skins and bones and such bits of driftwood as the sea might wash up.

For in this climate, shelter is more urgent than food. The Eskimo (or Inuit, as he calls himself) caught in a blizzard could freeze to death within hours. He found a way of using the snow around him to build a shelter with incredible speed; here he could survive for days without food, waiting for the storm to pass.

The snow house melted with the coming of spring, but another northern shelter, the *quarmang*, had foundations of stone that have lasted for centuries. Each summer the inhabitants would leave, taking with them the roofs of animal skin, and each winter the first families to return would spread their skins over the whalebone frames, add snow for insulation and settle in. Other northerners made simpler shelters using only earth and driftwood.

Summer brought long days of sun and signalled another way of living as families moved to new hunting and fishing grounds. The tent made of caribou or seal skin became the standard protection against the elements. Tents were built in many different ways and some northern peoples even lived in them all winter, much like the Indians further south.

The dwellings of northern peoples have always impressed travellers with how much was done with so little, and with how clever the simple can be.

Inuit snow goggles against glare

Bitterly cold, lonely and dark, the Arctic landscape in winter is a forbidding desert

of snow-covered land, jagged rock and icy seas. The igloo alone provided shelter.

"Igluvigak"– the snow house

Snow houses were the typical dwelling of the central Inuit in northern Canada. We call them "igloos" but the Inuit call all houses "igloos" and call the snow house "igluvigak."

They look as modern as space capsules and as old as the setting sun. Cut an orange or a globe in half and turn it flat side down? It's not quite that easy. Snow houses are built from the ground up. They require the windpacked snow that is found on the tundra. This is harder and more densely packed than the *taiga* snow that falls in the woodland areas further south. Like the hair of caribou, tundra snow traps air which acts as insulation to keep out cold. The snow must also come from a single snowfall so there will be no layering or cracks or differences in density.

The dome shape of the snow house is the secret of its success as a northern dwelling. It has neither a roof that has to be held up with posts or beams nor walls for the wind to push against. In the south, hurricane winds can blow down barns and houses or lift them up and away. But as the Arctic wind sweeps over and around the snow house, it moves downwards, pressing the walls further into the ground. In this way the curved surface uses wind pressure to make the building stronger.

A small snow house for emergency overnight shelter can be built in as little as an hour by two hunters caught in a storm or by one hunter in two hours. In it a person can wait out the storm for days without food by "thinking small," not moving, using little energy, a little as animals hibernate. No wonder it has been called "the most ingenious shelter in the world."

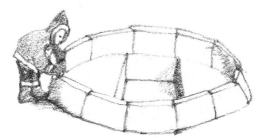
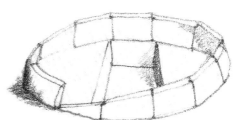

How the snow house is built

To build an igloo, an Inuk needs only a snow knife and tundra snow.

All snow houses begin the same way.

1. A circle is marked in the snow.
2. The first few blocks are cut from the center. These measure about a yard or meter long, two feet wide and half a foot thick, and weigh about 40 pounds or 18 kilograms. Each block is laid on edge (not flat like a brick) on the ground following the circle.
3. The tops are shaved off at an angle sloping upward and slanting inward.

4. The next row of blocks is then laid, each block tilting inward slightly to narrow the circle. Rows continue to be laid in a spiral up towards a dome. These spiraling rows support the dome and prevent the walls from caving in.
5. The keystone, or last block, is placed from the outside, but fitted from inside. Joints are chinked with snow.
6. A low entrance tunnel is cut near the bottom of the shelter, so low that a person must crawl to get inside. The tunnel floor is about one foot lower than the inside floor and serves as a cold trap.

A snow house may be so small it will barely allow a person to lie down or stand up. But an *igluvigak* can also be built much larger in a series connected by passages. Here large families may spend the whole winter with each unit serving a different purpose. The main living space is always built higher than the entrance tunnel which keeps out the cold. A platform built even higher for warmth is used for sleeping, working and cooking.

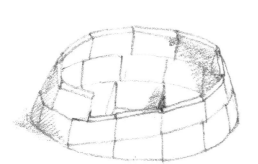
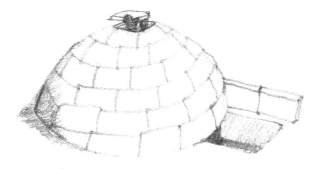
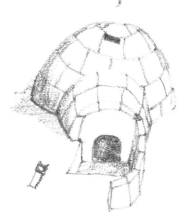

7

Igloos strung together could shelter a large family all winter. Even grandparents

had their own igloo. Smaller domes served to store meat, blubber and clothing.

Living in snow houses

The way air behaves seems to have been understood by all northern peoples and they used that knowledge to keep their dwellings warm.

They knew that hot and cold air do not mix as if stirred with a spoon. Nor does air move down and back up the way people go in and out of tunnels.

Cold air is heavy, so it stays down. In a tunnel it acts as a trap, stopping more cold air from coming in and warm air from going out. Warm air is lighter, so it rises. That means the warmest area in a snow house would be closest to the dome.

To make use of that warm area, the Inuit constructed a platform of snow along the back half of the dome. The small amount of heat coming from the human body or from a little soapstone lamp using blubber for fuel and moss for a wick collected here. The platform became the living and sleeping area.

Some igloos were lined with skin and this acted as additional insulation and stopped icicles from forming. Platforms covered with furs might be warm enough for babies to play on undressed during the day.

Snow walls are translucent; that meant any light outside managed to brighten the inside. Some igloos also had windows cut above the entrance tunnel; these were made by replacing snow blocks with seal intestine or a slab of clear freshwater ice. The tunnel entrance would be closed with a large snow block at night.

To strengthen the snow house, the women sometimes lit several lamps to melt snow on the ceiling. The lamps were then extinguished and the igloo was allowed to get cold enough for the wet roof to harden into ice. Such snow houses could be so sturdy that people and polar bears have been photographed on top of them.

When several snow houses were built and connected for family living, each would serve a special purpose: one might house parents and children, another grandparents

soapstone oil lamp

soapstone cooking pot

who often kept a favorite grandchild with them. An aunt and uncle and their children might occupy another unit. Smaller igloos served for refrigeration and storage. Dogs were never allowed inside except to give birth and nurse their puppies.

Only in northern Canada among the central Inuit did the snow house become the winter-long shelter of families. Such igloos were usually built on the beach, with their backs against slopes or cliffs, never on windy high ground. Elsewhere through the Arctic small snow houses were built as shelters against blinding blizzards or on offshore ice to allow seal-hunting through scattered breathing holes. This could be dangerous, especially if the shelter were built far from shore too early in winter when the ice field could be broken up by a storm.

Explorer B. Tenness described a snow house breaking apart while he was sleeping inside. The snow blocks gave off sounds like pistol shots as they came apart; the walls split from ceiling to floor, water poured in and rose close to the sleeping platform. Another occupant, stepping down to relight the lamp, shrieked as icy slush rose knee-high. They were fortunately able to wait until daylight when they cut a hole through the back wall of the igloo and escaped with their belongings to a safe place beyond the reach of the tide.

The Inuit were not afraid of cold. Children played outside in the coldest weather. Warm spells in winter were far from welcome, for they created other problems. When the top layer of snow melted and refroze, grasses were trapped under the hard surface and the caribou could not get at them. If the caribou starved, an important source of food was lost.

Arctic people built not just with snow but with whatever was handy. In the Western Arctic — from Alaska to northwest Siberia — driftwood washed up on the shores of rivers and seas was put to use. In Greenland, Labrador and the Eastern Arctic where there was almost no wood, shelters were made of skin, stone and whalebone. All tribes moved to tents in summer.

snow knives of wood, ivory and bone

bow drill for boring holes in wood, stone, ivory or bone **11**

Families returned each winter to use the old stone foundations of the *quarmang*.

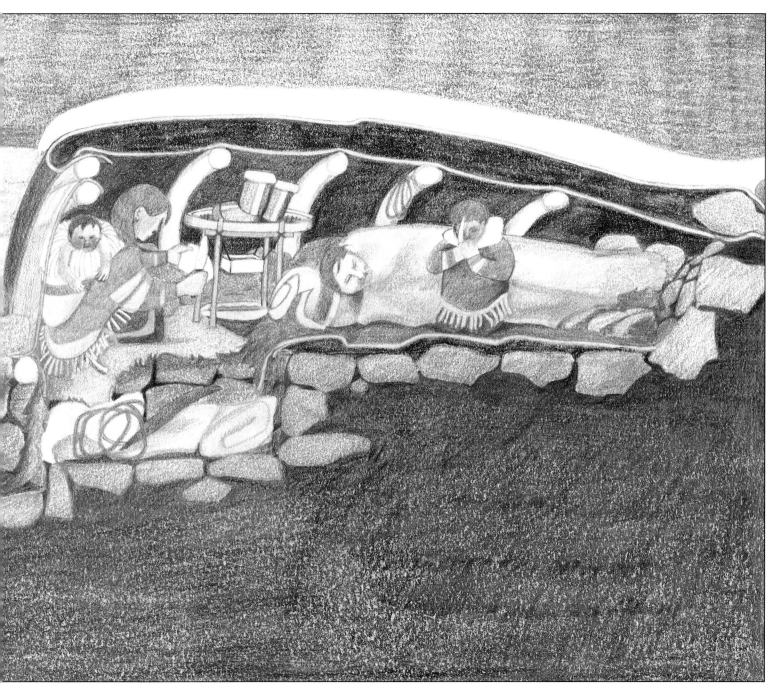

The whalebone frames were covered with skin and insulated with brush and snow.

Shelters of stone, skin and whalebone

The *quarmang* or *quarmak* may be even older than the snow house. These were built in Greenland, the Eastern Arctic, Baffin and other islands of the High Arctic. In contrast to the snow house that melted with the coming of spring, the foundations of *quarmang*s seemed to last forever. Thousand-year-old foundations can still be seen today.

Whales were once plentiful in northern waters. Hunting for them in small boats on open seas was dangerous but worth the struggle. One big Greenland whale could feed a whole village for a season, and its bones provide a framework for the roofs of dwellings.

The *quarmang* was usually built into the side of a hill. A ditch 20 feet or six meters long and about a yard or meter wide was dug sloping upward and lined with heavy stone slabs. This tunnel, which ended with a step up into the dwelling space, resembled the cold trap of the snow house. The living area also had a foundation and low walls of stone or bone. The roof was made with whalebone or, if available, wooden poles. Animal skins were stretched over this and then covered with a thick layer of brush for insulation. Then came more skins which were held down in the corners with rocks. A layer of snow added even more insulation. A window of semi-transparent seal intestine might let in light.

The building of *quarmang*s declined after the thirteenth century as the climate of the High Arctic grew colder during what is known as ''The Little Ice Age,'' and forced families to move further south.

14 *stone hammer with bone handle*

root pick with ivory bit

The Alaska sod-house

In Alaska, where driftwood was found along the shores of seas and rivers, it was used along with earth to construct a winter dwelling. It resembled a house as southern people know it except it was built partially underground, a pit dwelling. The floor and walls were framed with wood, and poles were used to hold up a roof of brush. All was then covered with earth. Outside the sod was shaped into a low rounded hill, so that wind would flow over it.

The sod-house used air pockets to conserve warmth much as the snow house did. A low entrance tunnel trapped cold air and kept it away from the living space; platforms were built for working and sleeping. Light entered these earth houses through a hole in the roof that also provided fresh air and let out smoke. This skylight was covered with skins at night or during storms. Two or three families might share a sod-house through the winter but they left it quickly as soon as spring came. Earth offered superb insulation against cold but it was useless against spring rains. Water seeped through and made the building too damp even for these hardy people.

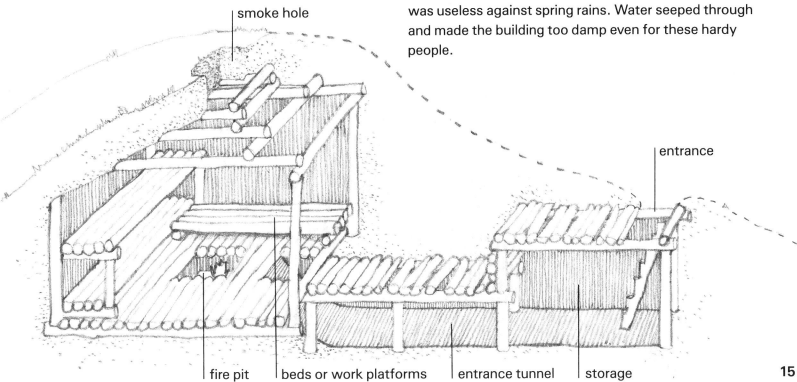

smoke hole

entrance

fire pit | beds or work platforms | entrance tunnel | storage

At winter's end, families moved to new hunting and fishing places.

Animal skins used to carry belongings were made into tents for summer camps.

Summer dwellings – tents of many kinds

When spring came the snow house melted and rain turned the sod house to mud. It was time for families to move and look for new hunting and fishing grounds. The skins that served as roofs or blankets through the winter became, first, carrying cases during the move, then tents for living in. No matter what housing was used in winter, the tent was the summer dwelling of all northern peoples.

In contrast to winter when the sun is never seen, there are days during the Arctic summer when the sun never sinks below the horizon. But it is never warm enough to melt more than a few inches of the rocky ground around the Arctic circle. Under that, sometimes as deep as a thousand feet, is *permafrost,* hard and waterproof as concrete.

No trees can grow on this tundra, but a surprising wealth of vegetation appears for a few short weeks in the constant sun. Some of these small plants and exquisitely beautiful flowers may be hundreds of years old, yet only a few inches high. They feed musk oxen and caribou which in turn became food for the people of the North.

The water's edge became a favored spot for summer settlements, as the sea teemed with fish, seal and whales and rivers filled with arctic char. Caribou or seal skin was used to make boats for hunting and fishing, as well as clothing and tents.

The tent of skin was the standard summer shelter of the North, but ways of building tents differed with different peoples.

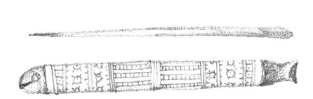

sewing needle and needle case

woman's knife

The *tupiq*

The tent of the Central Arctic Inuit came in many designs but still resembled the snow house in plan. If wood could be found, it was made into frames and posts. Otherwise whalebone or antlers that had been straightened were used. Sealskin was then stretched over the frame. The bed was placed at the back but not raised and no tunnel to stop cold entering was needed in summer.

In the tent design shown below, two pairs of poles were set up, one pair at the entrance and one pair at the edge of the bed. Then two cross strips were attached forming a roof ridge. Behind the poles at the edge of the bed, six or eight other poles were arranged in a semicircle. A large covering of sealskin was stretched tightly over this area. To allow light to enter, the front half of the tent was made of thin strips of skin or membrane. The entire tent was held in place by heavy stones.

The door was formed by overlapping one piece of skin with another to keep wind from blowing into the tent. One stone kept the tent flaps closed.

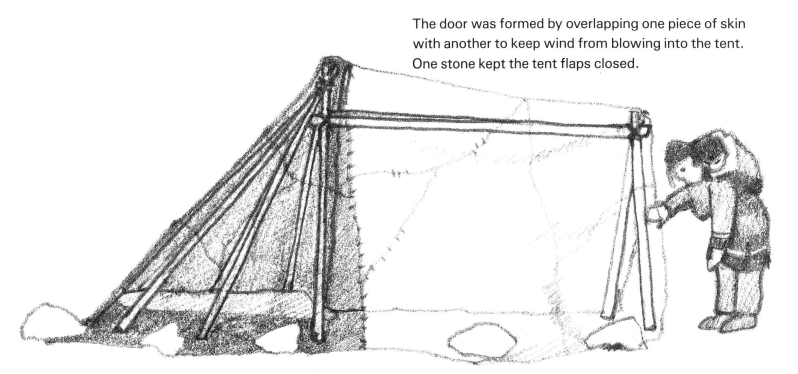

In summer the edges of seas and rivers were the favored sites for tent settlements

as families gathered to fish and make good use of the long daylight hours.

Other tents

Further north and west, another type of tent was used which needed only three poles. One strong tall pole was set up at the entrance and one at the back of the tent. A leather cord was then run over the top of both poles and fastened to stones on the ground. All was then covered with skin. The third pole was placed leaning against the entrance pole to support the door flap. If no wood was available, the poles were made from walrus bones, spliced together.

Some tribes converted their summer tents into winter dwellings by covering them with shrubs for insulation and then adding a second skin cover. When this was done, snow walls were built around the tent to protect it from the wind.

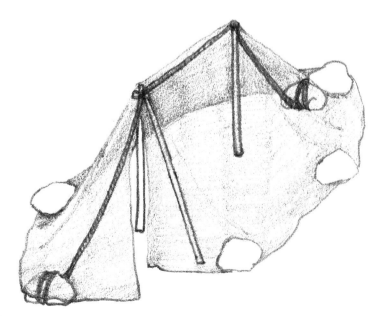

Today few northern peoples live in the kind of dwellings described in this book. But the snow house is still built for emergency shelter by those caught in storms and survival kits still give directions for its construction. Tents remain the popular shelter of the Inuit during the summer fishing season.

The major concern today in the Far North is pollution. The Arctic environment is very fragile. Plants grow very slowly and are easily destroyed. Winds carry pollutants vast distances from southern industrial areas and from northern Europe. Oil spills endanger sea and bird life.

Scholars have long been fascinated with how well the native shelters of the North met the needs of the people who lived there, and how the native people learned to live in ecological balance with nature and let nature work for them. The snow house for all its simplicity has been called ''the most sophisticated of native dwellings'' representing ''the most complete union'' of human beings with the environment. With the exception of the stone foundations of the *quarmang*, all northern shelters decomposed, returning to the vast, magnificent land from which they had come, neither changing nor damaging it.

Although the Inuit now live in modern structures, hunt with rifles, travel on snowmobiles and fish from motor-boats, some traditional ways and values persist and a surprising number still know how to build a snow house.